STEFANIA CAMPANELLI

HOMEOPATHY

THE VALUE OF INTEGRATIVE WELL-BEING IN OUR HANDS

© 2022 Therapeia S.r.l.
346 Via degli Abeti - 61122 Pesaro
www.gruppotherapeia.it
info@gruppotherapeia.it
ISBN 978-88-946926-1-7

INDEX

CODIFIED COMPOSITIONS, RULES OF INTAKE, PRECAUTIONS

HOMEOPATHIC CURIOSITIES

CONCLUSIONS

BIBLIOGRAPHY

PRESENTATION

Stefania Campanelli's concept of life is, simply, in a word, Holistic!

In her doing, in her study, in her life, she always has the heart of existence in mind!

And so, in life, as in her profession, she is dedicated to healing the conflicts of others' existences, with an approach ranging from speech to therapeutics, grounded in the study of the person as a whole.

From her, the Client/Person receives that help that is not easy, nor usual to find!

Science and Wisdom but suffused with a Love that few have and can convey!

Dr. Maurizio Annibalini

INTRODUCTION

There is no such thing as a perfect man; there is a man in search of perfection that is sometimes imaginary, ephemeral.

There is no such thing as a well-balanced man but rather one who, like a tightrope walker, exposes themselves in their first performance after years of practice; there is no such thing as a *pure* man, because purity would not be seen if there were not its opposite and contrary.

Each of us travels a road and encounters other beings, other souls also headed to their own personal path. We travel on parallel and/or opposite roads, along this path we are tested, *first of all* **toward ourselves**, and in such a case, sometimes, this awareness escapes by reflecting in others our own disharmonies, fears and misunderstandings; secondly, **toward others**, and *here*, clashing with the reflection of our own essence, with our own blocks, closures and in the affirmation of the *truths* that belong to us, we accomplish great things.

The mind *echoes* the more direct and less mediated expression of the soul, as an individuality, manifesting the latter's disturbances in a mechanism of *synchronicity*, as a higher concept than the simple cause/effect relationship typical of traditional medicine (e.g., I am sad and I necessarily get sick), in a vision of simultaneity of time and meaning, which features the body, which is nothing but *me* in the manifestation of an emotion.

I feel an emotion and simultaneously, at the same instant, the body, which, I repeat, is nothing but *me*, does the same thing, in the form of another matter.

Illness itself becomes an interpreter of a different transition and transformation from one state to another, illness, then, as a possibility to look deep inside each of us and watch what happens during the synchronic event between mind and body.

In this vision, unconventional, or rather *integrative*, medicine becomes the spokesperson for change, understood as the possibility of modifying lifestyles and ways of life, until then considered impossible. The person appears as the center in a *space*, the body, where pain is located and as the *manifestation* of an illness (acute, sub-acute, chronic), in a space/time relationship representative of the inseparable partnership between psyche and soma.

Unconventional medicine finds its strength in reading *beyond the lines*, going beyond the physical or mental symptom, in a concept of healing that stems from the transmutation of disease, focusing on what is *lacking* so that one becomes more *complete* and healthy.

Homeopathic medicine considered as *divine* word and the body as a *miracle* are representative of a totality, the organism, which is often able to trigger a self-healing mechanism.

Homeopathic remedies act in a mechanism of action, designed to restore the functionality of the deficient organ, within its natural limits.

Homeopathy enables the renovation of freedom as a concept of *health* (health from Sanskrit *sarvas*: whole, entire, complete) by expanding the consciousness of those who approach unconventional medicine.

The person who understands how they get sick will embrace the disease with more tools, using a different conceptual approach to embark on their own healing journey.

Men have always defined their entire existence in search of an image of *Oneness* as a *quality of presence*; a difficult and sometimes complicated journey where they will have to avoid falling into unspoken *polarity*.

OUTLINES OF THE ORIGIN AND HISTORY OF HOMEOPATHY

"Where the spirit suffers, the body also suffers."
Paracelsus

Homeopathy, the science of observation par excellence, has its origins in the medicine, religion and philosophy of classical antiquity: evidence of its application can be found in the Bible, Sanskrit poems, Persian and Oriental culture.

The most important written notes were even found in Egyptian medicine (2700 B.C.), and the earliest evidence of a behavioral ethical medical code, dates back to the 17th century B.C., in Mesopotamia, the Code of Hammurabi. It should be pointed out that medical practice was in the hands of priests and therefore linked to supernatural mystical practices.

However, it is necessary to wait until the third century B.C. to see basic homeopathic principles enunciated by the Greek physician **Hippocrates of Chios** (430 - 370 B.C.), considered the father of medicine.

Hippocrates based his medicine on two basic principles: the principle of contraries (*contraria contrariis curentur*) and the principle of similars (*similia similibus curentur*).

He applies the former, when the cause of the illness is known, and the latter when it is unknown, focusing on the individual reactions of the sick person: "fever is suppressed by that which produces it and produced by that which suppresses it."

Taking up the philosophical concepts of **Empedocles** (484 - 421 B.C.) and **Alchemeon** (540 B.C.), **Hippocrates** emphasizes how the *soma* represents a unitary totality, whose health corresponds with the state of equilibrium between *humors* and organs.

Even **Galen,** his successor, who favored the principle of contraries, did not disdain to apply that of similars.

Likewise, Arab medicine knew and applied the principle of similars (Averroes: "Not every cure is made with its opposite".)

Ancient physicians applied the principle of similars as much as the principle of contraries.

Between the fifteenth and sixteenth centuries, a new figure appeared in medicine; Philippus Aureolus Theophrastus Bombastus von Hohenheim known as **Paracelsus**, a great thinker, physician, scientist and alchemist.

With **Paracelsus** we begin to talk about medicine of correspondences. Medicine is based on the physics of terrestrial bodies (philosophy), the study of the movements of the heavens (astrology) and the study of the psychisms of matter (alchemy).

He asserts that nature is the teacher of the physician who must, through experimental observation, understand the symptom, translate and interpret the universal order, through the indivisible *lens* of two entities; the macrocosm reflected in the microcosm.

After **Paracelsus**, **Giambattista Elmonzio**, **Tommaso Campanella**, **Linnaeus** stated the same principles which lead today to a holistic view; *"Disease is cured by disease."*

We can see how the principles of homeopathy have found continuity throughout the millennia in every civilization up to the present day.

It is with the German physician **Samuel Hahnemann** (1755-1843) of Meissen, Saxony, that we speak of modern homeopathy.

S. Hahnemann, father of homeopathy, graduated in Medicine from the University of Vienna. He was an eclectic personality in the medical and scientific fields, soon disillusioned with the sketchy and unscientific methods of his time. He knew ten languages and in order to support his large family he then devoted himself to the sole practice of translating.

In 1791 **S. Hahnemann** came across a text by a certain Cullen that dealt with Materia Medica, specifically a pharmacology text. He noted that *china*, bark of a Peruvian shrub of the genus *Cinchona*, if taken by healthy people, could induce the same symptoms as malaria and at the same time noted, thinking back to Hippocrates and the law of *similia similibus curentur*, that *china* itself also contained a mysterious substance that could cure malaria itself.

S. Hahnemann elaborated from the above experimentation a fundamental theory; *only by observing the effects of drugs on the body we can understand how to use them.*

With this in mind, a new scenario opened up for **S. Hahnemann,** namely, to eliminate from the substances that can be used as remedies even at minimal doses, the poisonous component through repeated dilution of the substances themselves.

As an excellent scientist and pharmacologist, he took care to always use perfectly pure remedies, which, despite dilution, might seem to have no efficacy left, but in truth took their healing energy from the original mother-substance.

Between one dilution and the next, **S. Hahnemann** would vigorously shake the resulting liquid; this molecular shock caused a reaction called *dynamization.*

In 1810 he published "*Organon of the Art of Healing,*" a work that stated the basic principles and description of the effects of a hundred remedies.

This was followed by the publication of *"Materia medica pura"* (1811-1821), a text describing in alphabetical order the set of symptoms caused by the administration in doses of a substance in a healthy individual and the individual remedies, according to the following parameters: description of the original source of the remedy, technique of preparation of the remedy, pathogenetic symptoms, onset and causality of the syndrome, psychism and psychosomatic changes, characteristic modalities, clinical indications, posology and dilution.

S. Hahnemann relying on the *principles of similars* and using drugs at high concentration, which, however, sometimes had aggravating effects, decided to move to a progressive dilution of the dose on a defined scale. This led to the discovery of the principle related to dosage, called the *process of potentization*, which represented a great contribution to therapy, without which the law of cure would have been forgotten.

As he himself writes:

"If simile acts upon simile, the result of this mutual action reveals itself in neutralization, annihilation of the original qualities and in production of another state, which is exactly contrary to the previous one. If the simile of the remedy acts upon the simile of the disease, the result of this mutual action is neutralization, annihilation of the original qualities, viz. of the pathopoiesis of the remedy and of the pathogenesis of the organism, and change into the contrary state, viz. health."[1]

In 1828, he published *The Chronic Diseases: Their Peculiar Nature and their Homeopathic Cure* in which constitutional types, tools of holistic integration between the disease and the sick person, were formulated.

---

[1] Raffaella Comito, *Introduzione allo studio dell'omeopatia*, second edition, Tecniche Nuove, 2000.

THE HOMEOPATHIC REMEDY, ITS VITAL FORCE AND ITS APPLICATION

"Medicinal virtue lies in herbs,
In woods, in stones, in minerals, in animals.
You (if your suffering will be light) without much difficulty
will be able to treat yourselves."

Francesco Chiari

"In the healthy condition of man, the spiritual vital force (autocracy), the dynamis that animates the material body (organism), rules with unbounded sway, and retains all the parts of the organism in admirable, harmonious, vital operation, as regards both sensations and functions, so that our indwelling, reason-gifted mind can freely employ this living, healthy instrument for the higher purpose of our existence."[2]

---

[2] Samuel Hahnemann, *Organon dell'Arte di Guarire,*, Edizioni Red, 1985.

In the painful knowledge of disease, men have researched possible causes of it and, over time, have led their thinking in multiple directions, methodologies and techniques.

Homeopathy - from the Greek *homoios* simile and *phatos,* suffering - is a medical science that aims to soothe suffering, cure and heal disease by acting deeply on the body, both in the short and long term; it is effective on humans, children, animals, and in agriculture and gardening.

A *holistic* methodology that treats the individual in his or her entirety with the goal of restoring the organic integrity and psychophysical balance of the human being.

It examines constitutional aspects, hereditary, emotional, traumatic, and environmental factors, and the ways in which symptoms of a disease manifest.

The body, mind, and spirit are linked in a concept of trinity, of connected and interdependent forces present throughout one's *journey,* as a basis for deciphering the notion of the life principle:

> *"...the unitary essence of human life cannot reside in the individual organ or tissue or cell or molecule or atom, but in the whole organism, the whole man."* [3]

---

[3] Samuel Hahnemann, *Organon dell'Arte di Guarire, Edizioni* Red, 1985.

The *Vital Force,* as **S. Hahnemann** called it, is an invisible, capable and intelligent guide that, together with other factors, regulates the body's self-defense mechanisms. It allows the body to be freed from blocked energy by limiting the damage of an illness that can result in an acute crisis. For example, a simple cold can be the way to eliminate toxic substances from the body, allowing it to regain its balance.

It happens, however, that the *Vital Force* also fails to reveal its efficiency, developing long-term chronic conditions in the body. Taking the example of the cold, in this case it could manifest itself with a repeated mechanism over time (one cold after another) resulting in chronic asthma.

At this point it is essential to look outside for help; homeopathy can be considered a viable answer.

The target of homeopathic medicine is not the disease but rather the individual who has been affected by it. The physical symptoms that manifest themselves in the mentioned concept of the trinity – body, mind and spirit - become relevant and it is important to note that they also appear in different ways in different individuals.

Homeopathy works on the potential of the *Vital Force,* an energy that will know how to direct itself well in a global relationship, which takes into account the forms under which the disease manifests itself in the individual parts (a concept far removed from traditional medicine, which turns its attention to the individual diseased part).

The symptom becomes, in this way, the protagonist, and its occurrence is an opportunity to select the appropriate remedy.

The homeopathic doctor observes, notes and tries to fit the symptoms into the framework of the needed remedy; notes the symptoms of the disease and the way they manifest in that person taking into consideration the person's physical constitution and specific personality.

The person, thanks to nontraditional medicine, deepens through the Doctor/Patient relationship the knowledge of their body, their *Self*, that intimacy of *being unique* and complete, in an image of unity and wholeness. Their consciousness expands, they listen and discover a new language, that of their body.

A person's comprehensive view of themselves and being able to describe the functioning of their body enable them to trace the deep meaning behind the specific language of each organ, which refers back to a set of universal meanings.

Homeopathic history, as in allopathy, considers family history as the starting point, followed by physiological, remote and proximate pathological history, and finally objective examination.

The characteristic of homeopathic consultation is rooted in the coexistence of the psycho-emotional factors or individual reactivity, concomitant with the disease.

Constantin Hering sums up the art of questioning in four dictates: listen, write, question, coordinate.[4]

- *Listening*: the patient shall tell their story, the homeopathic doctor will avoid interrupting or suggesting answers, and if necessary, he or she will try to direct the discourse to the circumstances and how the pathology evolved.

- *Writing*: it will be noted by the homeopathic doctor what is reported by the patient, and what was observed by the doctor.

- *Questioning*: homeopathic questioning requires time, patience and availability (not less than 45 minutes). It respects the emotional intimacy of patients (shy or taciturn, whose trust must be gained, or who talk too much, in either case they should be tactfully solicited one way or the other). Direct questions will be avoided, nor will requests be made that pose only two alternatives (yes-no).

- *Coordinate*: the homeopathic doctor should enhance and organize the symptoms.

Following the history and examination, the homeopathic doctor will consider what type of therapy to apply and may consider various types of treatment; either homeopathic only, using *simillimum* or a similar remedy that covers most of the symptomatology, or a drainage remedy, or using the combination of homeopathy and allopathy.

------

[4] Raffaella Comito, *Introduzione allo studio dell'omeopatia*, Tecniche Nuove, 2000.

It should be noted that there may be cases of patients who will not be able to be treated homeopathically. It should be remembered that homeopathy does not cure all diseases, as it is a reactive medicine that relies on the body's ability to respond.

The person (patient) during the homeopathic visit is respected in their essence, and their body becomes a symbol of a *living temple*, the body as a ritual place.

THE FUNDAMENTAL PRINCIPLES OF HOMEOPATHY AND THE HOMEOPATHIC METHODOLOGICAL SCHOOLS

"The macrocosm and microcosm are built on the same plan....
All the powers in the universe are already ours."

Swami Vivekananda

Just as the universe is moved by *fundamental principles* in harmony with other realms, homeopathy's *basic principles* are in balance with nature.

In order to better understand the *fundamental principles* of homeopathy, we will briefly enunciate those that at a current glance can best explain homeopathy as a science of nature, where the *principles* that govern it are in harmony with the pre-established laws common to the whole universe:

<u>CURE</u>: *Similia similibus curantur.*
Healing starts from the top down, going from the inside out, from the most important to the least

important organ, and symptoms disappear in the reverse order of their appearance.

ACTION:
Every action is matched by an equal and opposite reaction.

QUANTITY AND DOSE:
the required quantity of a drug is inversely proportional to its similarity.

QUANTITY:
the quantity of the action necessary to cause any change in Nature is as small as possible. The decisive dose is always a minimum, an infinitesimal.

EMPLOYMENT:
the dose and quantity that will diffusely and deeply permeate the organism, and imprint on it its essential mark on the vital force is that which will stimulate the functional sphere of the individual.

BIOLOGICAL DEVELOPMENT:
function creates and develops the organ.

DISEASE DEVELOPMENT:
functional symptoms determined by the vital force are in direct relation to the severity of the disease. Functional symptoms precede structural changes.

EXPERIMENTATION:
1) Any substance that in its natural state touches vital

energy, but to a small extent, will give rise to experimentation only when administered at high potency.

2) Any substance that in its natural state alters life energy giving rise to functional manifestations should be experienced only in its raw state.

3) Any substance that in its natural state disturbs energy by giving rise to destructive-type manifestations should be administered only in a potentized form.

<u>REPETITION</u> (concerning experimentation):
Never repeat the dose while symptoms determined by the previously taken dose still exist.

<u>REPETITION</u> (concerning therapy):
Never repeat a chosen remedy as long as it still continues its action in the body. "[5]

Unraveling the thread of *scientia,* which means knowledge, starting with the fundamental principles of homeopathy and focusing on the principle of similars, which *applies* to many complementary disciplines, different schools of thought gradually formed over time that became actual Schools (**S. Hahnemann** favored the administration of a single remedy at a time, identified according to the clinical picture of the sick person to be treated):

------

[5] Herbert A. Roberts, *Omeopatia. I principi e l'arte del curarsi,* Ed. Mediterranee, 2003

- the _unicist school_ is based on the administration of a *single* homeopathic *remedy* for life, which the subject will take, should a health problem of any kind occur. The Unicist Homeopathic Doctor seeks the *simillimum* through the analysis of manifested symptoms (physical, emotional and mental) regardless of the clinical diagnosis expressed. This method is used by the Anglo-Saxon school of the American **Kent** and the Italian **Negro** and **Galassi**.

- The _pluralist school_ is based on prescribing *multiple remedies* to be taken individually or in combination, following a set sequence. It developed as a result of the belief that the unicist school could not treat all patients. We mention the Italian **Lodispoto**, **Santini**, **Masci**.

- The _complexist school_ is based on taking several homeopathic remedies combined into a single preparation, the *"homeopathic complex"* whose foundation assumes synergy between the elements in action with each other[6] .

---

[6] Maurizio Annibalini and Donato Virgilio, *Summa Homeopathica*, Nuova Ipsa Editore, Palermo, 2015.

THE PATIENT, TYPOLOGICAL ASPECTS IN THE ANALYSIS OF CONSTITUTIONS, AND THE CONCEPT OF DIATHESIS OR MIASMS

> *To heal our relationship to our bodies is to heal our relationship with the Earth. To regain our ground is to regain our aliveness, and the foundation of all that follows.*
>
> *Anodea Judith*

Before going into the study of constitutionalist theory, it is important to understand the deeper meaning of "constitution" in homeopathy and trace its origins in the models (Greek and Italic schools) theorized until today: the constitutions of **Hippocrates**, the four biotypes of **Claude Sigaud** and **Allendy**, **Pende**'s model, and **Martiny**'s model.

Not all individuals are exposed in the same way to every disease, here is where the observation of the patient (person) takes on *absolute* significance, since morphological, physiological, intellectual, emotional, relational and pathological aspects indicate each individual's responsiveness to disease and way of experiencing the state of health, in a constant and unchangeable basis that is the genetic component given by the chromosomal heritage of the family of origin.

The need, therefore, to bring subjects together in groups, noting their fundamental aspects in a constant variable, related to the adaptive and reactive capacities of the environment, has been felt since ancient times.

The study of *constitutions* is an opportunity to analyze the transition from the state of health to the state of disease, and to activate preventive action accordingly with systematic therapy, based not on the disease but on the person.

What, then, is the *constitution?*

It is "what a *person* is,"[7] i.e., the set of those exclusive traits that differentiate one individual from another.

Here is that, for example, a longilinear subject possesses different characteristics from a brevilinear one, peculiarities that will accompany both, forever.

To better understand the main specifics of each subject we will use a *guide,* which is practical and will lead to an overall understanding in the classification and division into five **Constitutions**:

1- Phosphoric, physical development characterized by a tendentially long-limbed stature, pale skin, oval/elongated face, hypotrophic musculature, flexed (hyper) articulacy, small bones, tapered and delicate hand, easy subject to fatigability.

---

[7] Maurizio Annibalini and Donato Virgilio, *op. cit.*

The *emotional aspect* of the *phosphoric* is represented by "closure," difficulty in coping with everyday life by favoring the need for delegation in doing, existential crises based on identity conflicts, idealization of loves, attachment to reference figures.

<u>Positive personality aspects</u>: empathetic, dreamer, sensitive and sentimental.

2- **Carbonic**, physical development characterized by a tendentially brevilinear (medium-low) stature, pale skin, round face, not particularly toned musculature with a tendency to fat infarction, rigid articulacy (hypo), coarse bone structure, square and mushy hand (in keeping with the climate), easily prone to overweight. The *emotional aspect* of the *carbonic* is represented by "self-doubt," repetitive mental laziness, the need to delegate in order to evade responsibility, and the need to build his or her own little garden of "tranquility."

<u>Positive personality aspects</u>: sociable, courteous, outgoing.

3- **Muriatic**, physical development characterized by medium-high stature, pasty and oily skin, round/square face, regular and harmonious musculature, discrete articulacy, medium bone structure, square and toned hand, easy subject to obesity on an exogenous basis. The *emotional aspect* of the *muriatic* is represented by "hate," behavioral excesses with relative fluctuation of sentimental extremes: passion, resentment, jealousy, vindictiveness and cruelty.

<u>Positive personality aspects</u>: good self-regard, bright and with high energy.

*4- **Sulfuric***, physical development characterized by a medium-athletic stature, elastic and dry skin, square/harmonious face, toned musculature, oppositional articulacy, medium/harmonious bone structure, regular-dry hand and powerful in grip, easy subject to food overload. The *emotional aspect* of the *sulfuric* is represented by "anger," difficulty in accepting social rules, problematic in accommodating what stands between their desires and their fulfillment.

<u>Positive personality aspects</u>: powerful, strong, outgoing.

*5- **Fluoric***, physical development characterized by normo-basic stature, thin and skin with little elasticity, asymmetrical face, hypotonic musculature, lax articulacy, nonsymmetrical and deformed bone structure (scoliosis-kyphosis), hyperlaxed and shifty hand, easy subject to underweight. The *emotional aspect* of *fluoric* is represented by "fear," perpetual indecision, anguish of responsibility, tendency to endogenous depression.

<u>Positive personality aspects</u>: good survival instincts, lively intelligence and ambition.

It is crucial to remember that belonging to one of the five constitutions helps to predict diseases, highlight tendencies, and consequently recommend a certain lifestyle (diet), but never to make an automatic prescription for a *constitutional remedy*.

Each constitution is, by contrast, influenced by *four homeopathic diathesis* in different proportions.

Thus, *diathesis* (modern term) has the ability to determine constitutional prevalence and manifest its pathological potential.

It is a "chronic reactive model" with developmental symptoms of the subject, a kind of predestination over time; one is what one becomes, what one was from birth and is shaped over time, by endogenous and exogenous factors[8] .

The *theory of diathesis*, or more exactly of *miasms*, comes from the logical studies of **S. Hahnemann**, who, attempted to give the medical practice of the time a scientific approach, overcoming all those superstitions that still tied the meaning of disease to the *esoteric* sphere.

Only a few types of disease were known, and there was no relationship or method of classification.

S. Hahnemann formulated an initial classification, basing his research on a different interpretation of diseases, turning attention to the individual's *reactivity* and not to the pathogen.

The aforementioned investigation showed the possibility of developing different types of diseases, for example, bereavement could cause a hysterical crisis in some, and a gastroduodenitis in others. It also explained how the same disease could change differently from person to person, due to the individual degree of *responsiveness*; in some, a condition evolved by becoming chronic or healing.

According to homeopathy, *miasm* or more modernly ***diathesis***, is therefore a person's original

---

[8] Dr. Maurizio Annibalini, handouts related to the lecture on *diathesis* given at SMB School - Italy, Ancona.

predisposition to a peculiar type of disease, typical of their constitution.

This altered condition of latent health is defined by **S. Hahnemann** as the cause of chronic disease and he gave it, precisely, the name *miasm*.

Its origin is hereditary but can also be acquired as a result of antinatural suppression of acute disease.

Miasm in Greek means stain, contamination (from the word *miasmein)* and indicates that chronic diseases result from this state of contamination of the body.

"Some diseases (even if cured) leave an imprint on the patient in the sense that they cause a change in his or her response to external stimuli." [9]

In the classification of *diathesis* **S. Hahnemann** introduced the notions of PSORA, SYCOSIS, LUESISM and TUBERCULISM (*diathesis* added by the French School).

PSORA, represents the reactivity toward toxic aggression: the body is able to move the problem away from the vital organs, channeling it to peripheral tissues such as the skin and mucous membranes (dermatitis, cystitis, etc...).

PSORA consists of hereditary and personal factors, describing the adaptive response following *first contact* with one's microenvironment, an attitude to protect one's identity, comparable to the survival instinct.

Everything that comes into contact with *us* goes

---

[9] Samuel Hahnemann, *Organon dell'Arte di Guarire*, Edizioni Red, 1985.

through a biological or emotional recognition and evaluation system.

If the evaluation is positive, the whole thing will be integrated into evolutionary processes as a new resource, otherwise it will be *naturally* removed or at least a protracted elimination process will take place.

PSORA translated into a graph, looks like a *ladder*, where the *first* step or *first contact*, moves further and further away from the original path.

Modifications and adaptive responses occur in the organism in every relationship related to situations, events or substances present during the life cycle, a continuous progression of conflict between humans and the environment.

In an identificatory reading of the exclusive qualities of personality, the behavior of the PSORA individual enacts physical and psychic attitudes designed to affirm and defend the self through an original reactive mode.

Regarding the symptoms we can talk about COMPENSATED PSORA and DECOMPENSATED PSORA: in the first case, the state of health is optimal, the organism enacts a defense and elimination reaction, the perceptual threshold is not reached, we therefore talk about asymptomatic PSORA; in the second case, the individual feels with greater or lesser intensity of discomfort and is in a state of illness, in this case we talk about symptomatic PSORA.

SYCOSIS describes the accumulation, the withholding of everything we live with, suffering it.

It is considered an *abnormal immune reactivity*, with alterations in the *retinal-endothelial system (SRE)* representative of an essential aspect of the immune response, a *filter* of all undesirable materials.

The occurred inability to eliminate pathogenic *noxae*, and the related tendency to accumulate, results in an inclination for forced coexistence with that which is withheld; the person is no longer able to remove the causes and/or consequences of negative and harmful events from themselves, responding in conscious (anxiety or depression) and at other times unconscious (neurosis) ways.

Inflammation, a situation in which immune reactivity comes into play, represents the body's response to external aggression.

Traditional medicine treats inflammation with anti-inflammatories, while alternative medicine, which aims to be *nonaggressive*, acts on the individual by stimulating his or her response, which will vary according to the particularities of the individual, as well as the type of pathogen.

The person with a *sycotic* attitude enacts somatic and psychic behaviors that channel into the inability to protect the original self, with accumulation of tension.

With regard to symptoms, we can talk about COMPENSATED and DECOMPENSATED SYCOSIS: in the former case, there is a refusal to take charge of the triggering situation (asymptomatic SYCOSIS); in the latter case, the individual has signs of chronic intoxication affecting various organic districts (symptomatic SYCOSIS).

PSORA and SYCOSIS are two peculiar aspects of the human being that have always coexisted together, permanently in conflict with each other, *reason, conscious* ENERGY-SYCOSIS (*I, DUTY, COERCION*), and

INSTINCT-PSORA (*EX, INSTINCT, EXTERNALIZATION*).

PSORA and SYCOSIS are the two *diathesis* that have as their common denominator the defense of life.

LUE (or LUESINISM), according to **S. Hahnemann**, is characterized by the disruption of rules, harmony and balance, with a strong destructive component.

Chronic disease is one of the key features of LUE; the body collapses and fails to rebalance vital energies; irreversible organ failure, sclerosis, dementia, neoplasms, emphysema appear.

The conflict between will and duty, and the lack of suitable compensations, undermines the value of instinct and amplifies the said conflict with the appearance of guilt.

The renunciation of affirming (PSORA) and defending (SYCOSIS) the self, positions the individual in the acceptance of the path toward the annihilation (LUE) of the self, a consequence of non-divisible interests and events[10].

The deep conflicts, in the person with Lue behavior, manifest themselves in physical and emotional attitudes that mark the progressive loss of function of organs and apparatuses, until the fulfillment of an ominous prognosis.

Regarding the symptoms, we can talk about COMPENSABLE LUE and DECOMPENSATED LUE: in the former case, it is spontaneous in the individual to correct the primary error through reflection on the

---

[10] Maurizio Annibalini and Donato Virgilio, *op. cit.*

deeper meaning of *being*, it is an opportunity to welcome *change*, to bring existential transformations, the awakening of the *instinct* subtracted from submissions; in the latter case, the subject renounces self-affirmation, with further subjugation and self-punishment.

TUBERCULINISM, which **S. Hahnemann** did not mention, was introduced by the Swiss **Nebel** and later developed by the French **Léon Vannier.**

The term Tuberculism (from the Latin diminutive of Tuber "excrescence"), does not refer to tuberculous disease, but as with all other diathesis, it is a *reactionary process.*

Vannier, in developing **Nebel**'s conception, writes, "*the tuberculinic individual is a person whose organism has undergone a true transmutation, due to the hereditary transmission they have had to endure. And this is not the tubercular disease, but a transformed terrain, which has been transmitted to them, a terrain eminently favorable to tubercular manifestations.*"[11]

Today, tuberculism means the *reactive mode* of an unstable subject, the variability of symptoms is its characteristic feature of which we distinguish between a *sthenic phase* with *mild* symptoms (peripheral venous insufficiency, neurovegetative instability, engorgement of lymph glands, etc.), and an *asthenic phase* characterized by so-called *demineralization*, to which

---

[11] Raffaella Comito, *Introduzione allo studio dell'omeopatia,* Tecniche Nuove, 2000.

deeper symptoms belong (bronchitis, pneumonia, excessive coldness, etc.).

We can say that the *vital force* of the tuberculinic subject is very low, therefore, his or her lifestyle should include certain precautions, such as avoiding sudden temperature changes, great physical exertion, unbalanced diets, and mental stresses, which tend to result in an inevitable deficiency of phosphorus, calcium, and magnesium.

The imbalance of the above minerals is typical in our time due to acid rain, overuse of additives and pesticides, which inevitably results in blood acidosis and subsequent *demineralization.*

Thus, *diathesis* is a pathological and psychological predisposition, an alternation in the search for quality-of-life balance that triggers a *chronic reactive model,* with developmental symptoms of the subject.

For **S. Hahnemann**, disease (complex of symptoms peculiar to the person) was related to the study of *miasms.* The remedy was identified by focusing attention first on the disease, then the patient, and finally the symptoms.

Treating patients, does not mean to give diathesis or symptomatic remedies to remove the "weeds," but we study and propose a remedy that I would say is a simillimum embedded in diathesis, which reclaims, changes, regenerates the soil, the diathesis[12].

---

[12] Dr. Maurizio Annibalini, handouts related to the lecture on *diathesis* given at SMB School - Italy, Ancona.

DISCOVERING THE POLYCHRESTS

The term *polychrest* derives from medieval Latin polychrestus - which serves many uses – it was used in old medicine and pharmacology to denote a substance with various healing effects; also defined as the remedy.

Polychrests *embrace* the universal human value, *portraying* the personality aspects of the subject and *integrating* the nuances of the softer colors of the person's psychic intimacy, to his or her anamnestic picture and allowing a view of wholeness with the study of the different phases, initial and final of symptoms. In the final stage often the symptoms of the remedies are similar to each other and it is difficult to distinguish them, the two extremes of a remedy are not always clear.

The study of polychrests, therefore, allows us to eschew stereotypical remedies and broaden our views to more therapeutic possibilities.

ARSENICUM ALBUM

Main appearance/feature: Physical loss

- <u>*Origin and effects*</u>

Simillimum is derived from a well-known poison, arsenic (arsenous anhydride).

It is used to treat both short-course acute diseases and long-term chronic problems.

It is employed, in particular, for the respiratory tract and the entire digestive system, including the intestines.

The remedy was tested by **S. Hahnemann** with 390 homeopathic observations.

- <u>*Main symptoms*</u>

It is typical of those who suffer from physical *restlessness*, agitation and anxiety, those who fear loneliness, or who feel exhaustion disproportionate to fatigue, those who are susceptible to colds, flu, asthma, food poisoning, digestive problems, burning pains despite being cold, with aggravation of symptoms at night.

- <u>*Emotional appearance - blocks and qualities*</u>

Insecurity on the physical level characterizes a psychic profile governed by the *fear* of poverty and misery that induces the person to a thrifty attitude, in the relationship with material security.

Another expression of physical *insecurity* is hypochondria, "*the fear of disease, is experienced with an excessive obsession with personal hygiene.*"[13], with the overuse of laxatives, to the point of having to control the fear of death.

The need for control leads the individual to be suspicious of the outside world (e.g., fear of being poisoned), taking refuge in the faithful security of the couple.

The person is characterized by a sense of practicality and order, and when the latter does not result in the need to create an accurate environment to relieve the anxiety he or she feels, it can become a positive aspect in precision tasks: accounting, handicrafts, the aesthetic sector.

Another qualitative aspect is the surprising attention to detail. They are sensitive to the nuances of people and life and careful not to hurt others (they fear offending others), they stand out for their faithfulness.

The subject *Arsenicum Album*, experiences anxiety in its most exaggerated expression with fear for the future, not as a young person, but only after being tested by life.

---

[13] Philip M. Bailey, *Psicologia Omeopatica. Profili di personalità dei maggiori rimedi costituzionali*, Salus Infirmorum, 2020.

ARGENTUM NITRICUM

Main appearance/ feature: instinctive, restless

- *Origin and effects*

Simillimum is made from a crystalline chemical, silver nitrate (also used in the preparation of photosensitive films), a silver salt that is toxic to humans, it does not exist in nature and it is obtained by dissolving silver in nitric acid.

- *Main symptoms*

It is the leading remedy for emotional states involving anticipation, agitation preceding a dreaded event, test or examination.

The person worries ahead of time about what, in fact, might happen, with a tendency to develop all kinds of fears: claustrophobia, agoraphobia (the obsessive terror of walking through an open public place such as a square), fear of catastrophic events (such as passing under a skyscraper that might fall), panic over any situation that involves a sense of vulnerability and exposure.

In the *physical* reading of the remedy, the subject cannot stand the heat, needs to urinate frequently and often suffers from diarrhea caused by the slightest emotion.

- *Emotional appearance - blocks and qualities*

Fear of an *Argentum Nitricum* mind involves states of nervousness, lack of self-confidence, fear of being abandoned and being alone, restlessness related to the need to quickly finish an action taken.

In the individual there is a strong urge to *"jump*

down, when they look from a certain height, from a window of the highest floor or from a parapet of a bridge"[14], not with suicidal motivation, inexplicably the unknown *intimate* part is revealed.

When the person is in psychophysical balance, all insecurities dictated by weakened psychic abilities will be transformed into *qualities*, the person will be bright, open and helpful, sharp and logical, quirky, sensitive to emotions and not swallowed up by them, characterized by childlike enthusiasm mixed with a kind of gaiety.

---

[14] Philip M. Bailey, *op. cit.*

Phosphorus

Main appearance/feature: boundless

- ***Origin and effects***

Simillimum is white phosphorus which is a toxic metal that occurs as colorless or yellowish-white crystals that are insoluble in water.

Phosphorus is considered the fuel of the body, it is found in the bone marrow, liver, germ cells and nervous system. When its action is disturbed, it produces *inflammation,* and following the increase of the inflammatory stimulus, it causes *hypertrophy* leading to *necrosis* resulting in *fibrosis* (hence some diseases: gastritis, nerve hypersensitivity, ulceration, paralysis, muscle spasms, etc...).

- ***Main symptoms***

A typical symptom is the burning sensation localized to the shoulders, along the spine at the dorsal level, at the palm of the hand.

Other characteristic symptoms are: cardiac disturbances, arrhythmias, tachycardias, or simple feeling of having the *heart in the throat*, sleep difficulties (short sleeps), fluctuating emotional states (the subject goes from excitement and affection to states of indifference), gums are usually reddened and bleed easily, nasal discharge streaked with blood, dry coughing fits (appearing before nighttime), profuse sweating all over the body, aversion to sweet foods, meat, salty fish, hot milk, tea.

- ***Emotional appearance - blocks and qualities***

The greatest difficulty is mutability and

evanescence; the *Phosphorus* individual has a tendency to superficiality, losing sight of the *lessons* of previous experiences; evasion from reality is their self-defense mechanism.

An escape from the *harsh* reality of life, from a weak *ego* untested in the maturity of being, unable to leave the childlike identity. The subject's poor self-identity lies in the identification of themselves with others, especially with their partner and parents.

Dispersion of thought, clouded mind, confusion, are the most common conditions.

Fear and anxiety are cumbersome *traveling companions* and friends of hypochondria, which often assails the individual in its darkest and most frightening form: the fear of a fatal disease.

The subject reacts with the greatest intensity to any feeling of fear he or she experiences.

The unevolved *Phosphorus* person has a tendency to be self-centered and disrespectful, with *"a inclination for vices and is particularly vulnerable to gambling."*[15]

The radiant and luminous aspects of the *Phosphorus* individual are unreserved joy and love, transparency of feelings and sharpness of emotions; generous, spiritual and good-humored, they imparted to others the innocence and value for ideals.

Naivety as strength and not weakness makes *Phosphorus* personalities shining stars; after all, the word Phosphorus means *light-bearer*.

---

[15] Philip M. Bailey, *op. cit.*

LYCOPODIUM CLAVATUM

Main appearance/feature: lack of power

- <u>*Origin and effects*</u>

Simillimum is made from a moss, Lycopodium clavatus (an herbaceous plant in the Lycopodiaceae family, known as *wolf's foot*), whose ground spores are used.

It is considered one of the most important remedies (usually prescribed as a long-term constitutional remedy), is one of the polychrests most studied by **S. Hahnemann** and the most widely used in homeopathy.

"There is nothing in man that Lycopodium cannot cure" (J. T. Kent).

It acts deeply on the liver, digestive system, uric acid, urea and cholesterol metabolism, kidneys and genital system, skin and mucous membranes, and nervous system.

- <u>*Main symptoms*</u>

The characteristic subject of the aforementioned *simillimum* usually comes from a coercive and rigid family environment, with great contrasts in parental figures, low affectivity; they are irritable and *grumpy* upon awakening, distrustful, they lack confidence in their own abilities, and are afraid of failure (fear transmitted by parents who were themselves *Lycopodium Clavatum*).

Typical symptoms are memory disturbance, flatulence and abdominal pain, heartburn, inordinate desire for sweets, throat irritation, lack of energy in the afternoon (4 p.m.).

- _Emotional appearance - blocks and qualities_

The sense of _powerlessness,_ of the _Lycopodium Clavatum_ subject, is masked by a relatively hopeful personality with a wishful thinking to use some _sort of power,_ which is why, they may become overbearing, opportunistic, domineering with dominance of reason over feelings, convinced that they are the best (e.g., arrogant intellectual) and do not like to be contradicted.

They fear loneliness but could take an attitude of detachment from everyone and everything if, faced with illness, they felt resigned and helpless.

They are afraid of failure and consequently suffer from anxiety before anything really happens (related to performance anxiety experienced in childhood).

Among the distinctive _qualities,_ the _benevolent_ nature stands out. High-energy _Lypocodium Clavatum_ subjects try to maintain harmony with everyone by attempting to please those they meet in their path, dispensing pleasure to all.

They are excellent and valiant salesmen (e.g., car salesmen) and influential business managers with large sums of money. Given their skills in dealing amiably with people, they reach positions at the top of power, thanks to healthy pride and self-assertion.

They are soft-hearted, hypersensitive subjects, capable of emotion, and are aware that much of their happiness depends on their loved ones, toward whom they will be forgiving and caring.

For this remedy, _Lycopodium Clavatum_ women should be mentioned. They do not try to hide their insecurity behind a bold self-image, remaining aware of their anxiety, even if it is disabling in some cases.

This state of mind often results in the fear of being an inadequate wife or mother; they are prone to nervousness and generally try harder to please people.

They are rather shy, helpful and ready to offer praise and assistance to others.

ANACARDIUM ORIENTALE

Main appearance/characteristic: dissociation between good and evil

- *Origin and effects*

Simillimum or Malac bean, is made from the dried fruit (oval shape, long, and black in color) of the tree, also called, *Semecarpus Anacardium*, native to the mountainous regions of India.

- *Main symptoms*

It is the remedy indicated for the subject who is in constant struggle between two wills (between the divine and the demonic).

The characteristic symptom is weakness of sensory perceptions and exhaustion after mental exertion, resulting in headache, memory loss before an important exam or test, fatigue or drowsiness after lunch, coughing caused by anger, calf cramps when walking or getting up from a chair, warts and sticky sweat on the palms of the hands, a fragility that affects making any decision, with great distrust in oneself.

The *psychic symptoms* emphasized by **S. Hahnemann**'s *"Doctrine et traitement homéophatique des maladies chroniques"* 1835, are clinical: despair, indecision, impression that the spirit is separated from the body.

- *Emotional appearance - blocks and qualities*

The limitation of the *Anacardium Orientale* individual is the constant negative state in which he or she lives, the dominant evil part prevails in the battle against the good and comes out bursting with obscene acts, insults and offenses.

The *Anacardium Orientale* individual is introverted, not very expansive, surly, amoral and cruel; they sometimes play the part of the *persecuted* by entering a vicious cycle of paranoia.

When the person is able to tame their instincts, their angelic side brings them closer to practicing meditation and rationalizing obsessive thoughts and impulses.

SULPHUR

Main appearance/characteristic: the stimulated or passionate self

- *Origin and effects*

Simillimum is derived from sulfur (associated with the *fire* element), which in its natural state is solid, yellow-orange in color; it exhales suffocating odors, typical of certain thermal waters and areas near erupting volcanic strata.

Sulphur is a fundamental constitutional remedy, thus suitable for treating a variety of problems, as long as the subject closely reflects the *Sulphur* type.

When *sulfur powder* is left in contact with the skin, it results in burning irritation. Because of this characteristic, and because of its healing properties, e.g. the elimination of toxins (through a mechanism of action that brings harmful substances to the surface - from the inside to the outside - of the skin), it has always been used in homeopathy in the treatment of skin problems.

- *Main symptoms*

It is the typical remedy of the person who feels weak and hungry around 11 a.m., those who are greedy for sweet foods, those who experience heat in the head, burning sensation in the soles of the feet (when the person is in bed, he or she seeks coolness), and those who suffer from itching especially in the mouth, lips, vulva, and anus.

- *Emotional appearance - blocks and qualities*

The *Sulphur* individual is, generally, passionate.

In his eager search for a *higher intellectual level,* deep communication, he or she tends to establish philosophical relationships, resulting into long and interminable predefined arguments, becoming boring.

A dreamer with no practical sense, he or she overlooks the details of the physical and emotional realities of those around them (e.g. a *Sulphur* husband who forgets his wife's birthday); they tend to be opportunistic, selfish and proud, unwilling to sacrifice their own comfort and pleasure.

They love autonomy: "*they want to have the freedom to do what they want, to say what they want and with whom they want.*" [16]

The *Sulphur* individual's liveliness can erupt into anger when their will is not recognized.

To be always up to the situation, they are capable of lying; they understand the need to have laws and regulations, but they are not too shy about breaking them if it suits them.

They weave their positive *inspiration* into life through intellectual creativity, dwells in romantic and zealous love, with a heart filled with poetry for beauty and human love, walks the world with contagious enthusiasm and volcanic brilliance.

They are optimistic and eccentric with an open, careful and generous character toward others.

The harmony of a *Sulphur* individual is able to transform simple culture into wisdom, "*they tend to*

---

[16] Philip M. Bailey, *op. cit.*

have a natural dignity that they see reflected in traditional values, such as honor, courage and charity." [17]

---

[17] *Ditto.*

NUX VOMICA

Main appearance/characteristic: charismatic seducer or warrior

- *Origin and effects*

Simillimum is made from the dried seeds of the vomica nut, which are rich in strychnine. The tree is of eastern origin and belongs to the *Loganiaceae* family (small oval leaves and flowers, the fruit is an orange berry, similar in size to an apple, with whitish flesh).

It acts on a wide range of pathologies.

- *Main symptoms*

It is characteristic of those who are hypersensitive to touch, noise, smell, irritable to music, food, clutter, for example they might get nervous if the door slams or a piece of cutlery falls.

Typical symptoms are nausea and vomiting, digestive difficulty due to the use of alcohol and heavy foods, regurgitation of gastric fluid, both mental and physical spasm of the intestines (alternating diarrhea and constipation), and tendency to insomnia.

- *Emotional appearance - blocks and qualities*

The nature of a *Nux Vomica* subject, is dominant, loves power, the ability to acquire it and exercise it.

Inhibited emotionality and hypersensitive temperament are reflected outwardly with attitudes of irritability and impatience.

The less evolved individual is oriented toward social respectability and material things; they use anyone, even exploiting their family in order to achieve the above purpose.

The archetype of their shadow side is the tyrant, selfish with the need to satisfy their basic needs: food and alcohol (Bacchus), smoking (Tobacco) and sex (Venus).

Fearless, agile in mind and body they keep their own destiny under control and does not follow other people's orders.

If they are faced with an opponent, their mission becomes to defeat them, and when they have done so, they have no grudge against them.

If a *Nux Vomica* subject ignores you, it is because you are unimportant.

The archetype of their positive side is the paladin, they follow a moral code and love to protect the fragile.

They are by nature, magnanimous and charismatic, instilling confidence without gaps or shortcomings in those areas where their intelligence and experience are most limited.

From a social point of view, they are worldly individuals.

CALCAREA CARBONICA (CALCAREA OSTREARIA HAHNEMANNI)

Main appearance/characteristic: stasis or need for security

- *Origin and effects*

Simillimum is obtained from a special type of limestone, found in the underlying layer of the oyster shell.

It is a great polychrest and is also among the constitutional remedies. It can be used as early as infants and early childhood and acts slowly and deeply.

- *Main symptoms*

It is the specific remedy for those who have a tendency to constipation, colds at the slightest changes in weather, coughs that appear during teething or coughs induced by taking cold drinks or cool places, pains to urinate after catching cold, belching or acid vomiting, erosive eczema of the soles of the feet, and neurological irritability, insomnia, and asthenia.

Simillimum is also used in ossification difficulties, such as slow growth.

- *Emotional appearance - blocks and qualities*

The weakness of the *Calcarea carbonica* individual is the slow and methodical way in which he or she deals with life's events and issues.

They dislike *changes*; their conservative tendency limits their conscious openness and results into mechanisms of closures and, at times, dullness; they seek emotional self-protection.

If feelings are hurt, it is easy for the *Calcarea carbonica* subject to resort to pettiness, enacting a petulant behavior.

They can slip into mental paucity and neglect of information.

Independence is not their peculiarity; they need support and reassurance, especially in the family.

The virtue of the *Calcarea carbonica* individual is *simplicity*.

Their needs of family life are concrete, with a desire to pamper and indulge in the pleasures of life: eating, drinking, walking etc. They have a sense of hospitality, sentimentality and an empathetic sensitivity (cannot stand cruelty).

On the positive side, the *grit* not peculiar to the *Calcarea carbonica* subject translates into the ability to resist (like the oyster that when *frightened* closes in its shell).

IGNATIA AMARA

Main appearance/characteristic: vulnerability and emotional intensity

- *Origin and effects*

Similimum is obtained from the seed of *Ignatia amara* or *Strychnos ignatii*, a climbing plant native to the Philippines, it belongs to the Loganiaceae family and is also known as *St. Ignatius' Fava*.

It is an emergency remedy effective in treating emotional problems, shock, trauma; it treats psychosomatic illnesses and calms mental and behavioral obsessions.

- *Main symptoms*

The typical symptoms of the *Ignatia amara* individual appear after emotional stress with consequent development of sensory hyperesthesia, neuromuscular spasms associated with depressive state, but also contradictory and paradoxical symptoms: mood swings, asthenia with empty feeling in the stomach when waking up, *lump in the throat*, migraine caused by strong odors (smoke, coffee, food aromas, etc...) associated with nausea and biliary vomiting, and punctiform pains.

- *Emotional appearance - blocks and qualities*

Emotional fragility is the most obvious characteristic of the *Ignatia amara* subject. When they are low in energy *"all emotions, anger, sadness, joy, love, fear, concupiscence, are felt by the Ignatia amara individual with a degree of intensity not found in any other type.*"[18]

They tend to repress negative and painful emotions, resulting in a tragic outcome of their *feeling* and intellect; the person becomes the emotion itself.

Hypersensitivity represents the difficulty in the long journey of experience; the pain of sentimental abandonment, parental insecurity suffered at an early age, unrequited love, an evocative memory of childhood result in panic, phobias, emotional fickleness with transitions from laughing to crying without a tangible reason.

The qualities of the healthy *Ignatia amara* subject are freedom from manipulations caused by repressed grief and anger, and freedom from defensive avoidance mechanisms of possible suffering.

In the above refinements of emotional independence, the person expresses a graceful, intellectually and aesthetically refined sensibility, representative of insight and acuity.

The *Ignatia amara* individual walks the world with passionate, vibrant and enthusiastic vivacity, they are passionate about poetry, metaphysics, anthropology, nutrition, health and esoteric sciences.

Most women when high in energy combine *"a delicate sensitivity with a strong sense of identity and adherence to a high code of personal ethics."*[19]

---

[18] Philip M. Bailey, *op. cit.*
[19] Philip M. Bailey, *op. cit.*

SILICEA

Main appearance/feature: graceful and assertive

- <u>*Origin and effects*</u>

Simillimum is pure silica extracted from rock crystal; it is a white, inactive, insoluble powder.

Prepared at high Hahnemannian dilutions, it becomes a very potent general-action medicine.

Homeopathic doctors prescribe it as a long-term treatment; it is very useful for treating purulent wounds and chronic infections as it causes the body to eliminate, and reabsorb, diseased tissues.

- <u>*Main symptoms*</u>

A typical feature is susceptibility to respiratory tract disease; sputum is often yellowish and purulent.

In general, symptoms include modest inflammations that generate pus and then degrade, abscesses that are slow to heal, chronic laryngitis, constipation, worsening intestinal parasitosis, related to moon phases, headache, symptoms that are slow to pass, especially in cold individuals who lack energy and vitality.

- <u>*Emotional appearance - blocks and qualities*</u>

The *Silicea* subject stumbles, in intellectual endeavour, where fear, irritability, and shyness rob him or her of the confidence to complete a task.

They have a tendency to *fixed ideas*, they are afraid of sharp objects and pins, however, they seek them out and use them; they suffer from dizziness and headache with cyclic pattern, moreover, they have difficulties in both physical and psychological reaction, towards long illnesses or towards great physical and mental efforts.

It is a common *type* and usually is female.

Stubborn and determined, she does not easily change her mind, yet lacking self-confidence, she turns out to be *delicate* mentally and physically, she is often *hit* by the unexpected events of life, by which she feels assaulted.

The tenuous sensitivity of the *Silicea* person is their strength, the expression of their *beauties*: refined, sharp, deep thinker, able to plumb their inner self in an intellectual sense. They know well what they believe in and what they want, they avoid vulgarity, dishonesty and brutality.

They love to associate with kind and sincere people and are incapable of becoming aggressive with those they love.

"They tend to reveal their private life only to close friends, whom they can trust while respecting the privacy of others even without being asked to do so."[20]

Even when having fun, they maintain self-mastery.

---

[20] Philip M. Bailey, *op. cit.*

SEPIA OFFICINALIS

Main appearance/feature: autonomy and women's empowerment

- *Origin and effects*

Simillimum, commonly called *Sepia*, is the thick blackish-brown liquid (or black ink) given off by a *cephalopod* marine mollusk (equipped with ten tentacles, lacking an outer shell, but provided with a skeleton called a *cuttlebone*).

The Cuttlefish evades danger (possible predators) by hiding in its ink.

Squid ink contains many minerals, amino acids, taurine, sepia melanin, trace elements and enzymes; in homeopathy it is considered a true nonspecific (not typical) hormone stimulant.

Its action not only affects the feminine sphere but it is particularly effective on the genital system during the various stages of a woman's life: puberty, menstrual period, motherhood, climacteric, and menopause.

- *Main symptoms*

Lack of tone is the defining characteristic of the *Sepia* person, accompanied by nighttime insomnia or awakenings with anguished cries, hair loss, spasmodic dry cough, headache, hepato-biliary disorders, constipation with hemorrhoids, uterine prolapse, vaginal mycosis, recurrent urinary infections, asthma or chronic bronchitis, and general asthenia.

- *Emotional appearance - blocks and qualities*

Stifling of independence is the psychic enemy of the *Sepia* subject's automatism, who risks compromising their true nature by becoming apathetic and lacking motivation.

The loss of contact with their *vital force* weakens the *Sepia* individual's physique and mind, leading them to laziness and indifference.

Crying becomes frequent and intimately contemplating deep feeling could develop in depressive states. It is not easy to distinguish a *Sepia* personality from a *Natrum muriaticum* one; an individual might in the course of life alternate both, *"for example, a Sepia officinalis woman may enter a Natrum muriaticum state after a bereavement, or a Natrum muriaticum woman may enter a Sepia officinalis state during pregnancy."*[21]

In self-respect, the *Sepia* person is free from the emotional constraints and prejudices of others, walks proudly and with head held high in the *jungle of life*, and protects his or her intimacy with a facade of healthy, so-called instrumental aggression (the noun aggressive in accordance with its etymological root, has retained a remarkable wealth of meanings, including positive ones: capacity for initiative, assertiveness, vitality and success).

In the *Sepia* woman is most developed the innate capacity of the *witch's ancient wisdom*, the use of intuitive faculties and the love for the mysteries of the occult; which enable her to investigate into psychic or mystical realities.

The *Sepia* person is well related to his or her body,

---

[21] Philip M. Bailey, *op. cit.*

they are in total harmony with it, and they express their sarcastic and minimizing spirit with a light and graceful manner.

The *Sepia* soul is portrayed in the woman with her femininity welcomed, loved and expressed.

The healthy *Sepia* woman experiences sexuality as a gift by deriving pleasure from it while fully respecting herself.

PULSATILLA PRATENSIS

Main appearance/characteristic: feminine origin, experiences emotions without stifling them

- *Origin and effects*

Simillimum is obtained from an herbaceous plant in the *Ranunculaceae* (*Pulsatilla Vulgaris*), also known as *meadow anemone* (delicate bell-shaped flowers with hairy, flower-colored leaves), it contains a poisonous alkaloid that irritates the mucous membranes of the skin.

It is a basic first aid remedy, but it is also a good constitutional remedy.

- *Main symptoms*

The *Pulsatilla* subject experiences the extreme variability of all physical and psychic manifestations and their alternation (mutability and contradictoriness of symptoms).

The pains appear and disappear, are widespread, and the affected person does not know how to locate them.

A characteristic sign is venous congestion and stasis, both peripheral and of the portal system.

The mucous membranes are affected by sub-acute inflammation with yellowish-green discharge, recurrent nasopharyngitis (despite dry mouth, the subject is not thirsty), bronchitis in the catarrhal phase.

Signs worsen with a high-fat diet and large meals, resulting in a heavy stomach and flatulent colic.

Skin diseases: skin *rash*, chilblains with itching that worsens with heat, cyanosis of the skin.

Physical symptoms change all the time.

- *<u>Emotional appearance - blocks and qualities</u>*

The *Achilles' heel* of the *Pulsatilla* person is emotional fickleness (less intense than *Ignatia amara*), they can become tense and constantly irritable; overwhelmed by shifting ideas, the intellect is considered a tool for satisfying their emotional needs and desires.

Usually, frustration and tension are externalized in the family with complaining, crying (crying is generally their response to emotional pain) and great mental upset (evanescent thinking).

Pulsatilla subjects must experience abandonment (of family members) before finding their individuality.

Pulsatilla individuals when they feel loved are at their point of strength and balance; they are able to be a loving mother or father and they become the meeting point of family love.

The *Pulsatilla* type, when high in energy, expresses a charming innocence in their way of catching the things of life.

They are sweet and accommodating at the same time.

They can become, as Dr. Maurizio Annibalini recalls, the "*Sweet and Compassionate Barbancey Old Woman.*"

THUYA OCCIDENTALIS

Main aspect/characteristic: guilt, emotional openness and escape from intimacy

- *Origin and effects*

Simillimum is made from the fresh, leafy branches, harvested in spring, of the plant called White Cedar or *Tree of Life*; it belongs to the *Cupressaceae* family, is found in parks and gardens, and is used to form hedges (ornamental plant).

It is a great remedy indicated for all acute inflammatory diseases with a tendency to become chronic.

Acts on all organs; central and peripheral nervous system, skin, mucous membranes, lymphatic system, endocrine system, reticuloendothelial system.

Used extensively for conditions resulting from drugs, antibiotics, or in long-term corticoid use.

- *Main symptoms*

The neuropsychic system is the protagonist of this remedy in identifying the primary symptom. The subject is dominated by a depressive-anxious state, experiences constant and unmotivated restlessness throughout the day, and is mentally fatigued.

The above psychophysical snapshot converts into clear physical symptoms both in the digestive system (spasmodic constipation, morning or psychogenic diarrhea, meteorism) and in the urogenital system (chronic and relapsing genital infections both bacterial and fungal).

- *<u>Emotional appearance - blocks and qualities</u>*

The insurmountable limit of the *Thuya* individual is *guilt*, which participates in *Thuya*'s self-destructive behavior.

The feeling of self-loathing leads the subject to *become big*, they have a tendency to retain fluids, generate *warts* and benign tumors with the same intensity as the thoughts they produce.

They tend to be easily afraid, they have difficulty finding words and they isolate themselves from conversations, and they are hyperemotional.

Thoughts are painfully persistent; the combination of the right brain hemisphere and intense emotionality can cause states of confusion.

Vulnerability, as a result of the extreme sensitivity of the *Thuya* person, turns, in the reticent subject, into anger, with both self-destructive and vindictive tendencies.

Thuya women tend to avoid contact and wear masculine clothing to protect their individuality.

Thuya's beauty is in the *wisdom* of painful experience and the ability to *let go*.

The incentive to be passionate about life restores to the person a wild, intuitive streak, a delicately refined innocence.

NATRUM MURIATICUM

Main appearance/feature: abolition of pain

- ***Origin and effects***

Simillimum is nothing more than ordinary (cooking) sea salt, which comes from the salt pans of the Guéranda Peninsula and contains only *sodium chloride*.

Sodium chloride is an essential element in the body, the breakdown and circulation of which contribute to internal homeostasis.

It is an important constitutional remedy that has a profound effect on emotions.

- ***Main symptoms***

Cold sores are a typical sign of the subject *Natrum Muriaticum*.

Natrum Muriaticum is the remedy of somatizations (a fitting, though extreme, example to better understand the meaning of this *Simillimum*, is that of the person who says: I can't do it... then they get sick to avoid doing it), we can therefore expect acute headache, fever, insomnia with ease of awakening at night, metrorrhagia, slimming and asthenia, depression caused by sorrows, nasopharyngitis and tonsillitis (in the child), asthma with characteristic coughing fits, palm warts.

- ***Emotional appearance - blocks and qualities***

At the core of a *Natrum Muriaticum* individual's pathology is emotional pain, out of which arises the fear of suffering, which is not always conscious.

A fear that makes the person avoidant even in

intimate relationships (the typical thought is: if I don't open my heart I won't suffer!).

Behind the aforementioned fear are then other emotional difficulties of *Natrum Muriaticum* subjects, which are common traits, such as: the need to please everyone, low self-esteem, tendency to avoid feelings by taking refuge in intellect, smiling and joking, keeping busy, positive thinking, and being a perfectionist.

Controlling feelings is another distinctive feature that symbolizes an emotional shield toward previous emotional wounds and opens the door to moralistic and religious evangelism.

The *key expression* for *Natrum Muriaticum* individuals is *"bottling up their emotions,"*[22] thus accruing constant internal visceral tension with a tendency toward depression.

When the person is knowledgeable, he or she develops a pride disproportionate to actual intellectual knowledge.

The healthy *Natrum Muriaticum* is free from previous emotional trauma, is affectionate, free from addictions, believes in themselves and has confidence in their own abilities, and is *deep* without slipping into hypersensitivity.

They feel no remorse and courageously engage in relationships with other people, *giving* without the need to please. Morality translates into respect for traditional values. *Natrum Muriaticum* people when

---

[22] Philip M. Bailey, *op. cit.*

high in energy are aware of their emotional limitations and have descended into the depths of hidden intimacies to arrive at a conscious quality.

73

PLATINA

Main appearance/characteristic: fanaticism, pride and haughtiness

- <u>*Origin and effects*</u>

Simillimum is made from *metallic platinum* foam, belonging to the *noble metal family*, is silver-gray in color, stainless.

- <u>*Main symptoms*</u>

The mental component as an etiology of the various symptoms is relevant and evident; traveler's constipation, spastic pain and cramps, both in the abdomen and limbs, migraine, facial neuralgia, nerve disorders of genital origin, dysmenorrhea and polymenorrhea, vaginismus and vulvovaginal hyperesthesia.

- <u>*Emotional appearance - blocks and qualities*</u>

Fear of imminent death, ghosts, and the possibility of killing someone are the most common terrors of *Platina* subjects.

Anxiety takes on an unbalanced image, where the fear of going mad as well as feelings of strength and superiority alternate. The *Platina* individual cannot handle too many stimuli and sees shutting themselves in their protective shell and secluding themselves as the only soothing solution. The difficulty with confrontation is expressed in *Platina* individuals by a tendency to laugh off serious matters. The healthy responsiveness of the *Platina* person is characterized by a pronounced and passionate sensitivity. Sexual desire, especially in women, gives them the opportunity to benefit from their acceptance of the feminine side, without the barriers of taboos and obstacles affecting the natural knowledge of their being Women.

75

MERCURIUS SOLUBILIS

Main appearance/feature: the forerunner (the harbinger of the gods)

- <u>*Origin and effects*</u>

Simillimum is made from the liquid metal mercury or its compound mercury nitrate.

It has an intense action on the endocrine system.

- <u>*Main symptoms*</u>

It is the specific remedy for inflammation of mucous membranes especially acute or chronic tonsillitis, acute or repeated rhinitis and rhinopharyngitis, epidemic parotitis, corneal ulcerations, broncho pneumopathies, asthmatic bronchitis, gingivitis, periodontosis, stomatitis and aphthosis, ulcerative colitis, genitourinary problems.

Other typical features of *Simillimum* include swollen glands, generous salivation, profuse sweating, and metallic taste in the mouth.

- <u>*Emotional appearance - blocks and qualities*</u>

The temperamental instability of the *Mercurius solubilis* subject, the change of mood, as rapid as the change of their thinking, the inability to endure predictability and routine, represent the difficulty of their mind, which often experiences disintegration.

Since they do not have a good relationship with the roots of the earth, they tend to live in the head, which is why they seem detached from everything and everyone, even from their body that knows the static nature of everyday life (the subject may live on leftover food, stay up late).

When the *Mercurius solubilis* individual's ego is full of Self, the person tends to abuse his or her ability to understand, seeking personal power, the more shadowy side manifested in the *magician* archetype.

The positive archetype of the *Mercurius solubilis* subject is the mythological figure of *Hermes*, the mediator between the inner and earthly worlds (heaven or the unconscious).

The person is able to *"momentarily suspend logical thinking and open his or her mind to subconscious and superconscious sources of information.*

Typically, this is done unintentionally, when intuitive acumen suddenly disappears and reveals itself unexpectedly."[23]

Many individuals learn to manage this gift by being able, voluntarily, to make this connection with the deepest area of their mind.

Deep meditations, mediumistic abilities and divination become integral aspects of *Mercurius solubilis* personalities.

----

[23] Philip M. Bailey, *op. cit.*

GRAPHITES

Main appearance/characteristic: gracefulness

- *Origin and effects*

Simillimum is made from a mineral coal, the *graphite* (also called plumbago or lead ore), dark gray in color, shiny and greasy; homeopathic preparation is by trituration (black powder insoluble in water and alcohol).

It is a remedy for chronic diseases, although it is not among the constitutional remedies, there are people who respond positively to its administration for most of their lives.

Graphite is commonly used for the production of pencil leads.

- *Main symptoms*

The hallmark of this remedy is skin disease: atopic eczema, hyperkeratosis, fissures, scars, keloids, periungual warts.

Also useful for endocrine disorders, and also disorders of the digestive system.

- *Emotional appearance - blocks and qualities*

The shadow side of the *Graphites* person is hypersensitivity to relational contrasts. When someone, particularly a family member, does not behave lovingly toward them, a whole range of negative emotions are unleashed in their inner self, setting in motion the mechanism of *"ruminating with such intensity that it results in a heavy black cloud all around them."*[24]

They will communicate their discomfort and anger by slamming doors or breaking dishes and crying in solitary.

Another personality aspect is indecision, especially when an emotion that can cause a state of distress prevails. This includes making even the smallest decisions.

The positive side is simplicity and kindness; the healthy *Graphites* individual can be concrete, realistic, refined and balanced.

Gifted with a special form of innocence, they tend to say what they think gently and without argumentative guile.

Sweet, empathetic (they care a lot about others), sensitive with keen intelligence, they are inclined to volunteer and participate in humanitarian activities.

---

[24] Philip M. Bailey, *op. cit.*

STAPHYSAGRIA

Main aspect/characteristic: controlled anger

- <u>*Origin and effects*</u>

Simmillimum is made from *Staphysagra* flowers, an herbaceous plant belonging to the *Ranunculaceae* family.

The flowers are lily-like in shape and are blue in color; it is also called a *knight's spur*.

It is a common plant in Mediterranean regions and it grows at the edges of fields.

The remedy was pioneered by **S. Hahnemann**, who devoted special attention to it and carried out the pathogenesis of *Staphysagra*.

Simmillimum acts on the nervous system (mental and neurovegetative) and demonstrates how a character behavior disorder can trigger a sequence of physical symptoms.

- <u>*Main symptoms*</u>

Staphysagria is indicated in the treatment of character disorders of harassment, humiliation, indignation, and suppressed anger, which generate psychosomatic manifestations: digestive disorders, pseudo-cardiac symptoms, low back pain, concentration and memory disorders, apathy, nighttime insomnia, dental and paradental disorders.

- <u>*Emotional appearance - blocks and qualities*</u>

Anger and resentment are the main emotional tensions that take command over the evolution of the *Staphysagria* personality, creating restlessness in the body and mind. This disturbance is felt as an explosion.

The deteriorated *Staphysagria* individual "*lives, eats and dreams wounds of vengeance.*"[25]

The individual fails to harmonize with a straightforward and safe daily routine because the repressed anger has to escape. As a result the person will tend to agitate, they will need to connect with the archetype of the *savage*, without taking into consideration the dangers in an attempt to achieve a state of excitement (e.g., extreme sports).

The opposite pole to anger is the gentleness of the subject *Staphysagria*, a mild, gentle soul, spontaneously helpful, idealistic, interested in spiritual themes, of witty intelligence, who loves to make themselves indispensable.

---

[25] Philip M. Bailey, *op. cit.*

LACHESIS MUTA

Main appearance/characteristic: apprehension and excitement

- ■ *Origin and effects*

Simillimum is made from the venom of the black rattlesnake, a yellowish or pinkish-backed snake that lives in the virgin forests of Central or South America.

It is a fundamental remedy, important in both occasional and long-term treatments.

It is also used for self-medication against throat afflictions and in problems related to the menstrual cycle.

- ■ *Main symptoms*

The main indication is irritation of the throat more pronounced on the left side or moving from left to right, irritation extending to the ears and sometimes to the back of the head, with swallowing difficult and more painful when passing liquid food than solid food.

Other indices are menopausal conditions, blood and vascular disorders (capillary fragility, thrombophlebitis).

Symptoms are pronounced upon awakening and warm weather.

- ■ *Emotional appearance - blocks and qualities*

The symbolism of the snake twisted on itself, which refers back to the remedy, is representative of the image of the human being's sexual energy, which must find an outburst so that it does not backfire on itself.

When the creative power of sexuality and passion does not find an expressive channel, the *Lachesis* person becomes tangled in jealousy (most often unreal), anger and selfishness, and may become irritable, tense, proud, intolerant of restrictions, paranoid, touchy.

Energetic sexual force, when intimately healthy, can be transformed into artistic flair, spiritual experiences, and ardent affirmations in professional and personal spheres.

The *Lachesis* individual moves in a vibrating energy, inspiring of the highest principle of wisdom (the art of healing others, in the emblem of the healing of the snake).

GELSEMIUM

Main appearance/characteristic: cowardice

- <u>*Origin and effects*</u>

Simillimum is made from the outer part of the roots of a North American plant called Virginia Jasmine or Yellow Jasmine.

The remedy acts mainly on muscles and motor nerves, but it is also used in the treatment of influenza.

- <u>*Main symptoms*</u>

It is the specific remedy for muscle aches accompanied by weakness, fatigue and chills, trembling and shivering, feeling of loss of control over one's limbs, fever with modest thirst but noticeable sweating, localized headache in the back of the head and heavy eyelids, anxiety about bad news, performance anxiety (exam, interviews, competitions).

- <u>*Emotional appearance - blocks and qualities*</u>

The complexity of the *Gelsemium* personality is to recruit body and mind, to make them ready for action and leave them in tension.

Mental fatigue is associated with muscle weakness, feeling unable to move, unable to walk through life.

When the mind is blocked the subject just wants to *be left alone* in their inner silence.

Intense fear from emotions and sorrows makes the individual vulnerable to such an extent that he or she triggers cowardice, fails to cope, and withdraws into himself or herself (mental and physical paresis).

The positive side of this *Simillimum* is the sensitivity to the conscious path, the individual knows their phobias, they know what limits and hostilities run through their unconscious, and, despite everything they act, they head toward the achievement of the quality of personal well-being.

CODIFIED COMPOSITIONS, RULES OF INTAKE, PRECAUTIONS

In a healthy state, the vital force that animates the organism reigns supreme.
Samuel Hahnemann, Organon (1810)

The body, the temple of soul and mind, is the means by which to experience life; through *matter* we create the relationship with the inner and outer worlds, a *whole*, a *unicum*, moving in the indefinite space of the search for knowledge.

Only by walking the path of body awareness we can truly understand our essence; sometimes, during the long journey, the body becomes ill or experiences certain alterations, without being able to independently activate the process of self-defense, it weakens and requires help from outside.

Homeopathic remedies can be that support, and in respect of the human organic substance, they can revive, with new impulses, the natural self-defense mechanisms.

Traditional homeopathic remedies are found

commercially in the form of *granules* and *globules* (smooth, white spherules consisting of a central sucrose core with overlapping layers of lactose), they are water-soluble and contained in tubes.

The *granule* has a weight of about 0.05 gram (50 mg), and 1 gram contains about 20, the *globule* weighs about 0.005 gram (5 mg), and 1 gram contains about 200.

A *tube-granule* contains 80 (4 grams), or 120, a *tube-globule* contains 200 (1 gram), confetti *tablets* (100 mg); glycerin *macerates* glycerin (50%), water (20%) and alcohol (30%); drops - 10 drops correspond to 3 granules; *potentiated capsules* and *homeopathic cures* of which there are 30 capsules containing both homeopathic remedy and placebo.

The outer label of the tube bears the name of the healing substance, followed by a number representing the dilutions made and two letters, the proportion of the dilution. For example, *Belladonna 5CH,* 1 part of the original substance was diluted in 100 parts water and alcohol, then vigorously shaken (succussion), this process was repeated five times.

In the final dilution there is only one trillionth of the parent substance of *Belladonna*!

Available doses are *4CH, 5CH, 6CH, 7CH, 9CH, 12CH, 15CH, 30CH, 200CH, 1000CH, 10000CH, 50000CH, 100000CH, 500000CH, 1 millionCH.*

There are also decimal dilutions, going back to the example of *Belladonna* we can have *D3, D4, D30* etc., whose modes of use are the same as the centesimal ones.

Thus, the combination of a (Roman) number with a letter indicates the energy, the *power* of the preparation.

The *granules* and *globules* should be made to be absorbed through the mucosa of the tongue (perlingual) or allowed to dissolve in the mouth; in the case of infants, it is recommended to dilute 3 granules in a tablespoon of water.

The dosage is the same in adults as in children, since homeopathy does not work by amount of substance present.

Generally, but not a rule, granules are used at low dilutions, for symptomatic remedies, and are also taken several times a day (3 granules at a time).

The *globules* are, on the other hand, used for so-called single doses, the whole tube-dose is taken, at longer intervals even every 7/10/15/21/30 days or more, at the discretion of the homeopath.

The precaution to be followed when administering homeopathic therapy is to take the remedies between meals (30 minutes before or after meals), this is because of the form of intake through the oral mucosa.

It is generally advisable to observe these times before taking any flavor (such as candy, various drinks, juices etc.).

The only drink allowed is water, because in theory it should be tasteless, odorless, colorless.[26]

Other precautions, such as taking mint, coffee etc., have been invalidated by recent studies and

---

[26] Valter Masci, *Omeopatia. Tradizione e attualità*, Tecniche Nuove, 2003.

experiments.

There are some remedies that should not be taken together or alternated such as e.g., *Apis* is the enemy of *Rhus toxicodendron*, *Ignatia* of *Coffea*, which in turn does not get along with *Nux Vomica*, *Belladonna* is opposed to *Dulcamara* etc. The list is endless, which is why knowledge and study of the remedies is as essential as being accompanied by an expert in homeopathy.

Side effects of homeopathic remedies are nonexistent.

Homeopathic remedies contain no drug substance and perform their action through energetic information from centesimal *dilution* and *dynamization* of the remedy.

The incongruous intake of the homeopathic remedy may, however, sometimes result in the so-called, *homeopathic aggravation*, which simply means, intensification of symptoms already present in the patient, or it may result in the onset of new symptoms, already present in the pathogenetic picture (*pathogenic aggravation*), or finally, *intrinsic aggravation* (improvement of symptomatology accompanied by the appearance of *eliminatory crises* e.g., diarrhea) may occur.

Silmillimum acts only on the *target*, that is, on the cells that have that specific alteration that needs that specific remedy.

Simultaneous intake of traditional medicines and homeopathic remedies is not contraindicated; no pharmacological interferences of any kind have been detected.

Other pharmaceutical forms include oral vials, suppositories, drops, tablets, ointments, and ovules.

Homeopathic medicines are produced following the standards of the French or German Pharmacopoeia; in many nations they are recognized and equated with other medicines and provided by the health care system, such as in Germany, France, Great Britain, and the United States.

In Italy, only a few years ago the name was changed from *homeopathic remedies* to *homeopathic medicines*, and production was regulated by Legislative Decree No. 185 of March 17, 1995.

HOMEOPATHIC CURIOSITIES

The key step that allows the basic substance to then be *homeopathically* processed, diluted and dynamized, and then become a *homoeopathic remedy* is the preparation of the Mother Tincture (M.T.), the manufacturing technique for which is described by the French Official Pharmacopoeia in 1983.

The starting substances, called *homeopathic stocks*, consist of:

1)   plant products
2)   mineral and chemical products

PLANT STOCKS

The plants used to make mother tinctures are derived from *wild cultivation*, that is, processed without chemical additives or pesticides; however, it would be preferable to use plants born wild in their natural habitat.

The French Pharmacopoeia specifies to use fresh plants to be used within forty-eight hours of harvesting;

dried plants are used only for exotic species that are difficult to find. The whole plant is used, as appropriate, such as belladonna (whole flowering plant), Calendula Officinalis (flowering tops), Valeriana Officinalis (roots)[27] .

HOW ARE MOTHER TINCTURES PREPARED?

The preparation of Mother Tinctures, is developed in six stages:
1- Phase of shredding the plant with firm cuts.
2- Weighing phase.
3- Maceration phase in stainless steel vessels with a well-calibrated hydro-alcoholic mixture (21 days of strictly cold maceration).

The ratio of dehydrated product to hydro-alcoholic mixture should be 1:10, that is, from 100 grams of dried plant, 1000 grams of mother tincture should be obtained.

With Calendula Officinalis the ratio is 1:20.

The grade, that is, the *alcoholic strength* of the mixture, varies according to the solubility of the active ingredients to be extracted.
4- Phase of collecting the decanted liquid and squeezing the residue with a pressure of about 100 bar.
5- Phase of mixing the two liquids and related resting phase for 48 hours.
6- Filtering phase.

---

[27] Valter Masci, *op. cit.*

The advantage of mother tinctures is that there are numerous active ingredients, but for this reason they are more delicate and keep less, unlike alcoholic tinctures, which keep longer because the ratio is 1:5, and the steeping time can be either hot or cold (steeping time 5-10 days).

MINERAL AND CHEMICAL STOCKS

Homeopathy extracts from the mineral world:
- *Pure elements*, such as phosphorus and gold.
- *Pure compounds*, such as silver nitrate and potassium phosphate.
- *Chemical compounds of natural origin*, sea salt or "*ostrearum limestone*" obtained from the oyster shell.
- *Synthetic chemical compounds*, such as Phenobarbital and Chlorpromazine.
- *Original mixtures* (fancy compounds), such as *Hepar sulfur*, with formula discovered by **S. Hahnemann**, composed of equal parts of *calcarea ostrearum* and sulfur flowers that are then heated in the crucible to red color.

Homeopathy derived from the mother tincture; the 1 dilution is called **1CH** where the letter **C** stands for *centesimal,* and the letter **H** stands for *Hahnemannian.*

Dynamization was homemade by holding the bottle in the hand; it was not until 1830 that Dr. Mure developed the first industrial machines.

The motion is important, it must follow a unidirectional path (vertical or horizontal) and it should also be abruptly reversed.

We will get 2 CH if to our 1 CH that we pour into clean bottle, we add, 70% parts alcohol and 30% water, at 70° and perform 100 percussions again, and so on. (Example: ARNICA 5 CH).

A BIT OF HISTORY ON MORE MODERN DILUTIONS/DYNAMIZATIONS

S. Hahnemann in the last years of his life worked on the sixth edition of the *Organon*, which was not published until after his death in 1921.

Within the text, S. Hahnemann described a new method for preparing homeopathic remedies; he used the 50-millesimal scale, rather than the centesimal scale, which had been used up to that time.

This allows for more practical, effective and *gentle* remedies at the same time.

This practice did not become widespread until the 1950s/60s, reaching its peak in the 1980s; today it is the mainstay of current homeopathic therapy for a certain section of unicist homeopaths.

Fiftymillimals (LMs) were devised by **S. Hahnemann** to avoid aggravations during homeopathic therapy thus, to have remedies that were more manageable and gentler in their action.

The basic substance is subjected to three centesimal triturations in lactose: 3^CH. 0.05 grams are taken that are diluted in 500 drops of hydroalcoholic solution (100 gtt. of 90° alcohol + 400 gtt. of water). One drop of this solution is poured into a bottle containing 100 drops of 95° alcohol. It is shaken 100 times. With one drop of this solution, you wet 500 lactose globules and you have the 1^LM, which is spelled, however, 0/1 LM (where 0 means globule).

Thus, first 1:500 and then 1:100 are the dilutions of the basic substance, that is, 500x100= 50,000 (fifty thousandths dilution).

One globule of the 1stLM is then dissolved in 100 drops of 95° alcohol and shaken 100 times. With 1 drop, 500n globules are impregnated and you have the 2^LM (both the solution and each of the globules).

So below, 1 drop in 100 drops, 100 dynamization, 1 drop in 500 globules.

Typically, 1 LM to 30 ML is used in drop bottles, or tube-globules.

These high degrees of dilution are used to move from ponderal doses to molecular doses and then to atoms only.

It is stated that homeopathy starts at 4CH and up.

In CH the ratio is 1:100, in LM 1:50,000. At the 1st CH there is a hundredth of the initial amount of substance, at the 2nd CH a ten-thousandth, at the 3rd CH a millionth. Up to the 4th CH there is still something of the ponderal of the basic substance, then there are only molecules; at the 9th CH the concentration of the homeopathic strain is 10^8, and thus much less than at the 5CH and that is 10 with 8 zeros= one hundred millionth more diluted. At 12^CH the concentration of the starting remedy is practically zero. 12^CH (or 23DH or 4LM) is the limit value beyond which there are no more molecules because the Avogadro's number is exceeded, which is 6.023x10-

23, and which represents the number of gram molecules in units of substance. 12 CH is precisely 10-24 so there is no more gram molecule of substance.

But there are biophysics that are demonstrable with sophisticated techniques (spectrophotometry, Raman laser, nuclear magnetic resonance). So not fresh water (=placebo), because in addition to dilutions there are dynamizations to consider. These impart particular electromagnetic characteristics to the solvent, creating hydrogen bridges between the water molecules in the solvent (H=O-H-H=OH) forming hydroxonium ions that take on peculiar characteristics, depending on the initial base substance.

Already **S. Hahnemann** in *Chronic Diseases* asserted that, with trituration and dynamization, some energy of the original substance is released. Energy that is then transmitted to the water and then to the water of the organism, whose responsiveness to disease it modifies. This modified, polarized, quantized water interacts with the biological water of the organism, providing for the substance-specific therapeutic modifications. Thus, the *simillimum* transmits biophysical, electromagnetic information necessary to restore the body's state of health. It is said that homeopathy is never wrong. The remedy, if right, works; it is us who prescribe, or the receiving organism, who are not in tune with the remedy. There must be a good "pair" match. It has been seen that these homeopathic remedies are inactivated by the metal detector and electromagnetic waves of cell phones, and not, as was said in the past, by taking mint or coffee.

Fast and coarse messages are transmitted at low

powers, slow and complex signals at high powers, intermediate messages at medium powers. Presence of the source stock prevails at low doses, whereas the memory or imprint of it prevails at high doses. Intermediate messages are transmitted at medium powers."[28]

---

[28] Maurizio Annibalini and Donato Virgilio, Summa Homeopathica, Nuova Ipsa Editore, 2015.

CONCLUSIONS

by Maurizio Annibalini

What emerges spontaneously is praise for such ability to come up with such fresh and new Homeopathic concepts.

In her initiation into Homeopathy Stefania Campanelli put all her fine, intellectual, intuitive, scientific and open energies into producing a very useful book for all!

And, for the experienced Homeopath, a "Cultural Revolution" - here's why:

The Remedy's choice to evolve boldly, in one's own individuality, toward a new and positive concept, disengaged from the classically understood introspection or evolutionary mode.

The VIRTUE OF the Remedy, of the Subject.

These are absolutely new concepts in Homeopathy, not so highlighted or never found in the Classical Medical Matters, and long desired by me too - finding the positive side of Remedies.

The ability to transform one's decisions, to choose whether, provided that pain is connected to life, to become a better person or a worse one. Whether to react with negativity or to know how to question oneself, and for example to transform the anger of certain Remedies into determination, strength, constructive work; and it is always the same Remedies.

The *Bottom Remedy* is not a condemnation. *Ignatia* is finally a person redeemed from the judgment of being strange and bizarre and specifically "refined intellectually and aesthetically, with insight and acuity."

This is the main body of the small and essential Work, preceded by a good historical-philosophical background and followed by notions of good Homeopathic practice.

A RENEWED HOMEOPATHY: that's what this book is all about, and thanks to Stefania!

Feb. 9, 2022, Dr. Maurizio Annibalini

BIBLIOGRAPHY

Maurizio Annibalini, Donato Virgilio, *Summa Homeopathica*, Nuova Ipsa Editore, 2015.

Philip M. Bailey, *Psicologia Omeopatica. Profili di personalità dei maggiori rimedi costituzionali*, Salus Infirmorum, 2020.

Rocco Carbone, *Compendio delle terapie naturali minori*, Edizioni Arte Scienza Evoluzioni S.r.l., 2004

Raffaella Comito, *Introduzione allo studio dell'omeopatia*, Tecniche Nuove, 2000.

Denis Demarque, Jacques Jouanny, Bertrand Poitevin, V. Saint-Jean, *Farmacologia e materia medica omeopatica*, Tecniche Nuove, 2013.

Thorwald Dethlefsen, Rudiger Dahlke, *Malattia e destino, il valore e il messaggio della malattia*, Edizioni Mediterranee, 2014.

Samuel Hahnemann, *Organon dell'Arte di Guarire*, Edizioni Red, 1985.

Robin Hayfield, *Omeopatia. Guida pratica al benessere quotidiano*, Vallardi I.G., 1996.

Anodea Judith, *Il libro dei chakra. Il sistema dei chakra*

e la psicologia, Neri Pozza Editore, 2020.

Valter Masci, *Omeopatia. Tradizione e attualità*, Tecniche Nuove, 2003.

Herbert A. Roberts, *Omeopatia. I principi e l'arte di curarsi*, Edizioni Mediterranee, 2003.

Gianfranco Trapani, Luisella Zanino, *Nozioni essenziali di materia medica omeopatica – rimedi di origine vegetale, minerale, animale e principali nosodi*, Tecniche Nuove, 2013.

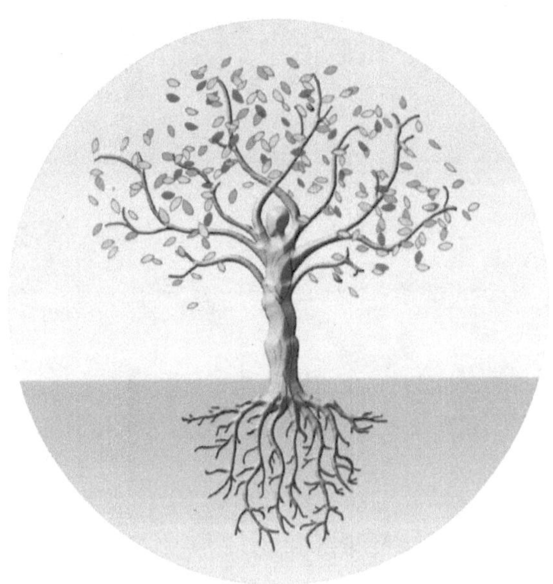

The person is not the disease
but is the possibility despite everything,
in a holistic vision that embraces man
his totality of body, mind and spirit

www.gruppotherapeia.it

www.ingramcontent.com/pod-product-compliance
Lightning Source LLC
LaVergne TN
LVHW091605170726
843492LV00007B/2274